THE GUITAR
3 Chord Songbook

PLAY 50 GREAT SONGS WITH ONLY 3 EASY CHORDS

ISBN 978-0-634-04994-1

For all works contained herein:
Unauthorized copying, arranging, adapting, recording, Internet posting, public performance,
or other distribution of the music in this publication is an infringement of copyright.
Infringers are liable under the law.

Visit Hal Leonard Online at
www.halleonard.com

Contact Us:
Hal Leonard
7777 West Bluemound Road
Milwaukee, WI 53213
Email: info@halleonard.com

In Europe contact:
Hal Leonard Europe Limited
42 Wigmore Street
Marylebone, London, W1U 2RN
Email: info@halleonardeurope.com

In Australia contact:
Hal Leonard Australia Pty. Ltd.
4 Lentara Court
Cheltenham, Victoria, 3192 Australia
Email: info@halleonard.com.au

Contents

Corrine Corrina
(Alberta Blues)

Words and Music by Bo Chatmon

© 1929 Robo Publishing, LLC
Administered by Spike Driver LLC
All Rights Reserved   Used by Permission

All Together Now

Words and Music by John Lennon and Paul McCartney

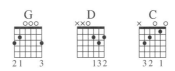

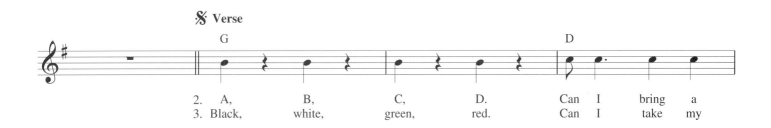

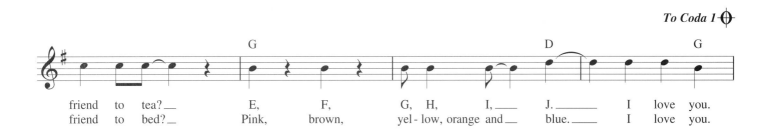

Copyright © 1968, 1969 Sony/ATV Songs LLC
Copyright Renewed
All Rights Administered by Sony/ATV Music Publishing, 8 Music Square West, Nashville, TN 37203
International Copyright Secured   All Rights Reserved

Chop the tree. (Bom, pa, bom.) Skip the rope. (Bom, pa, bom.)

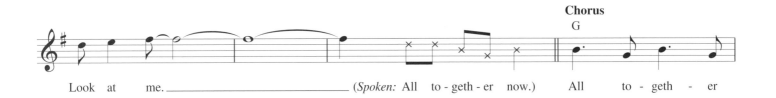

Look at me. _____ (*Spoken:* All to - geth - er now.) All to - geth - er

now. (All to - geth - er now.) All to - geth - er now. (All to - geth - er now.)

All to - geth - er now. (All to - geth - er now.) All to - geth - er now. (All to - geth - er now.)

(All to - geth - er now.) All to - geth - er now. (All to - geth - er now.)

All to - geth - er now. (All to - geth - er now.) All to - geth - er

now. (All to - geth - er Bom.) All to - geth - er now. (All to - geth - er Bom.)___

All to - geth - er now. (All to - geth - er now.) All to - geth - er now. (All to - geth - er now.)

D.S.S. al Coda 2

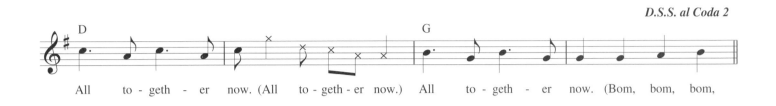

All to - geth - er now. (All to - geth - er now.) All to - geth - er now. (Bom, bom, bom,

⊕ **Coda 2**

now. (All to - geth - er now.) All to - geth - er now. (All to - geth - er now.)

All to - geth - er now. (All to - geth - er now.) All to - geth - er now. (All to - geth - er now.)

All to - geth - er now. (All to - geth - er now.) All to - geth - er now. (All to - geth - er now.)

All to - geth - er now. (All to - geth - er now.) All to - geth - er now. (All to - geth - er now.)

All to - geth - er now._____

All Apologies

Words and Music by Kurt Cobain

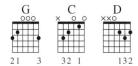

Intro
Moderately

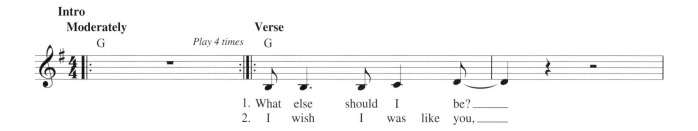

Play 4 times

Verse

1. What else should I be? ____
2. I wish I was like you, ____

All a - pol - o - gies. ____   What else should I say? ____
eas - i - ly ____ a - mused. ____   Find my nest of salt. ____

Ev - 'ry - one ____ is gay. ____   What else should I write? ____
Ev - 'ry - thing ____ is my fault. ____   I'll take all the blame, ____

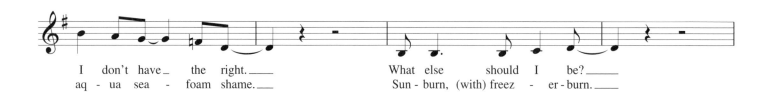

I don't have ____ the right. ____   What else should I be? ____
aq - ua sea - foam shame. ____   Sun - burn, (with) freez - er - burn. ____

© 1993 EMI VIRGIN SONGS, INC. and THE END OF MUSIC
All Rights Controlled and Administered by EMI VIRGIN SONGS, INC.
All Rights Reserved   International Copyright Secured   Used by Permission

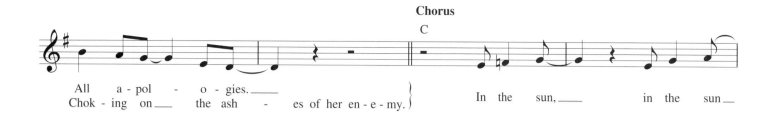

All a - pol - o - gies.____
Chok - ing on ____ the ash - es of her en - e - my. In the sun, ____ in the sun ____

____ I feel ____ as one. ____ In the sun ____ in the sun... ____ (I'm)

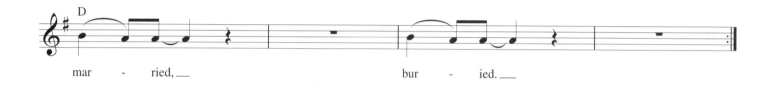

mar - ried, ____ bur - ied. ____

Mar - ried, ____ bur - ied, ____ yeah, yeah, ____ yeah, yeah. ____

Outro

____ All a - lone ____ is all ____

Repeat and fade

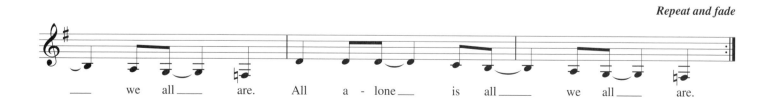

____ we all ____ are. All a - lone ____ is all ____ we all ____ are.

All Shook Up

Words and Music by Otis Blackwell and Elvis Presley

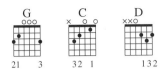

Copyright © 1957 by Shalimar Music Corporation
Copyright Renewed and Assigned to Elvis Presley Music
All Rights Administered by Cherry River Music Co. and Chrysalis Songs
International Copyright Secured   All Rights Reserved

I love best,__ my heart beats so it scares me to death! When she touched__

Outro

__ my hand, what a chill I got.__ Her lips are like__ a vol -

ca - no that's hot! I'm__ proud to say that she's my but - ter - cup. I'm in

love! I'm all shook up.__ Mm,__ mm, ooh, ooh, yeah,__

__ yeah,__ yeah!__ My __ yeah,__ yeah!__ Mm,__

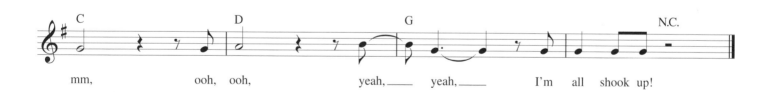

mm, ooh, ooh, yeah,__ yeah,__ I'm all shook up!

Additional Lyrics

2. A well, my hands are shaky and my knees are weak.
I can't seem to stand on my own two feet.
Who do you thank when you have such luck?
I'm in love! I'm all shook up! Mm, mm, ooh, ooh, yeah, yeah, yeah!

Bridge My tongue gets tied when I try to speak.
My insides shake like a leaf on a tree.
There's only one cure for this soul of mine.
That's to have the girl that I love so fine!

The Ballad of John and Yoko

Words and Music by John Lennon and Paul McCartney

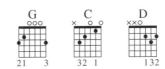

Verse
Moderate Rock

1. Stand-in' in the dock at South-amp - ton, try'n' to get to Hol-land or France.___
2.-5. *See additional lyrics*

___ The man in the mac__ said,__ "You've got to go back."__ You know they

did - n't e - ven give us a chance.__ Christ! You know it ain't eas - y,_____

you know how hard it can be.__ The way things are go - in'__

1.

5th time, To Coda

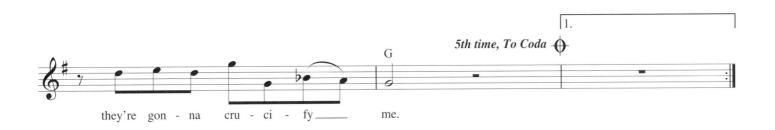

they're gon - na cru - ci - fy_____ me.

Copyright © 1969 Sony/ATV Songs LLC
Copyright Renewed
All Rights Administered by Sony/ATV Music Publishing, 8 Music Square West, Nashville, TN 37203
International Copyright Secured   All Rights Reserved

3. Drove from

Sav - ing up your mon - ey for a

rain - y day,___ giv - ing all your clothes to char - i - ty.

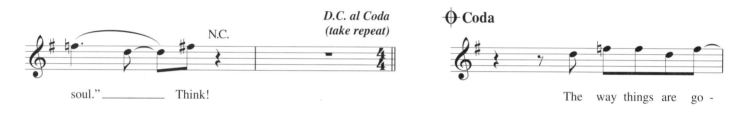

Last night the wife said, "Oh boy, when you're dead, you don't take noth - ing with you but your

soul."_____ Think!   The way things are go -

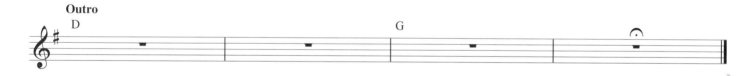

- ing___ they're go'n' to cru - ci - fy ___ me.

Outro

Additional Lyrics

2. Finally made the plane to Paris,
Honeymoonin' down by the Seine.
Peter Brown called to say, "You can make it O.K.,
You can get married in Gibraltar near Spain."
Christ! You know it ain't easy.
You know how hard it can be.
The way things are goin'
They're gonna crucify me.

3. Drove from Paris to the Amsterdam Hilton,
Talkin' in our beds for a week.
The news people said, "Say, what're you doin' in bed?"
I said, "We're only try'n' to get us some peace."
Christ! You know it ain't easy.
You know how hard it can be.
The way things are goin'
They're gonna crucify me.

4. Made a lightnin' trip to Vienna,
Eating choc'late cake in a bag.
The newspapers said, "She's gone to his head;
They look just like two Gurus in drag."
Christ! You know it ain't easy.
You know how hard it can be.
The way things are goin'
They're gonna crucify me.

5. Caught an early plane back to London,
Fifty acorns tied in a sack.
The men from the press said, "We wish you success.
It's good to have the both of you back."
Christ! You know it ain't easy.
You know how hard it can be.
The way things are goin'
They're gonna crucify me.

Barbara Ann

Words and Music by Fred Fassert

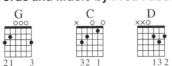

Intro-Chorus
Bright Rock

Ba - Ba - Ba - Ba - Bar - bara Ann.   Ba - Ba - Ba - Ba - Ba - Ba - Bar - bara

Chorus

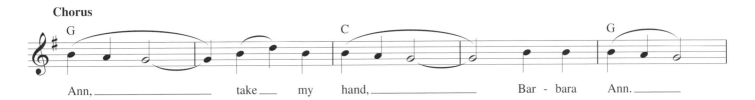

Ann, _____ take ___ my hand, _____ Bar - bara Ann. _____

You got me rock - in' and a roll - in', rock - in' and a reel - in' Bar-bara Ann, Ba - Ba - Ba -

To Coda ⊕ **Verse**

- Bar - bara Ann.   1. Went to a dance, look - in' for ro - mance. Saw Bar - bara Ann, so I
  2. Tried Bet - ty Sue, a - sides Bet - ty Lou, tried Mar - y Lou, but I

Chorus

thought I'd take a chance.   Bar-bara Ann, Bar-bara Ann, take my hand. Oh, Bar-bara Ann, Bar-bara Ann,
knew she would-n't do.

take my hand. You got me rock - in' and a roll - in', rock - in' and a reel - in' Bar-bara

1st time, D.C.
2nd time, D.C. al Coda

Ann, Ba - Ba - Ba - Bar - bara Ann.

⊕ **Coda**
Outro   *Repeat and fade*

Bar - bara Ann, Bar - bara Ann. _____

© 1959 (Renewed 1987) EMI LONGITUDE MUSIC and COUSINS MUSIC INC.
All Rights Controlled and Administered by EMI LONGITUDE MUSIC
All Rights Reserved   International Copyright Secured   Used by Permission

Can't You See

Words and Music by Toy Caldwell

Verse
Moderately slow

1. Gon - na take a freight train down at the sta - tion, Lord.
2., 3. *See additional lyrics*

I don't care where it goes. Gon - na climb a moun - tain,

the high - est moun - tain. I jump off, no - bod - y gon - na know.

Chorus

Can't you see, whoa, can't you see what that

wom - an, Lord, she been do - in' to me? Can't you see,

can't you see what that wom - an, she been do - in' to me?

D.C. al Coda

Coda

Oh, Lord.

Interlude

D.S. and fade

Can't you

Additional Lyrics

2. I'm gonna find me a hole in the wall.
   I'm gonna crawl inside and die.
   Come later now, a mean old woman, Lord,
   Never told me goodbye.

3. I'm gonna buy a ticket, now, as far as I can.
   Ain't never comin' back.
   Grab me a south bound all the way to Georgia now,
   Till the train it run out of track.

Copyright © 1973, 1975 Spirit One Music, A Division of Spirit Music Group, Inc.
Copyright Renewed
International Copyright Secured   All Rights Reserved

Be-Bop-a-Lula

Words and Music by Tex Davis and Gene Vincent

Chorus
Moderately

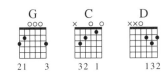

Well_ Be - Bop - a - Lu - la, she's my_ ba - by. Be - Bop - a - Lu - la, I

don't_ mean_ may - be. Be - Bop - a - Lu - la, she's my ba - by. Be - Bop - a - Lu - la, I

don't_ mean_ may - be. Be - Bop - a - Lu - la, she - e - 's___ my ba - by

doll, my ba - by doll, my ba - by doll. ___ 1. Well, she's_ the _ girl in the

Verse

2. *See additional lyrics*

red _ blue _ jeans, ah, she's the queen_ of ___ all __ the _ teens.

Ah, she's the wom - an ___ that I _ know, _ ah, she's the wom - an that

Chorus

loves_ me so, say. ___ Be - Bop - a - Lu - la, she's my _ ba - by.

Copyright © 1956 Sony/ATV Songs LLC and Three Wise Boys Music
Copyright Renewed
All Rights on behalf of Sony/ATV Songs LLC Administered by Sony/ATV Music Publishing, 8 Music Square West, Nashville, TN 37203
International Copyright Secured   All Rights Reserved

Be - Bop - a - Lu - la, I don't_ mean_ may - be. Be - Bop - a - Lu - la, she -

- e - 's_ my ba - by doll, my ba - by doll,_ my ba - by doll,_ let's rock.

Guitar Solo

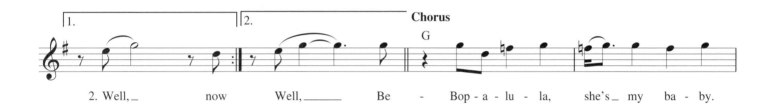

2. Well,_ now Well,_ Be - Bop - a - lu - la, she's_ my ba - by.

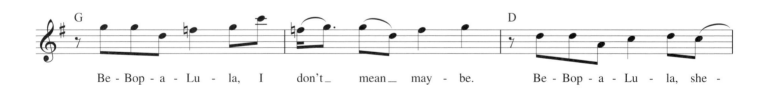

Be - Bop - a - Lu - la, I don't mean_ may - be. Be - Bop - a - Lu - la, she's my_ ba - by.

Be - Bop - a - Lu - la, I don't_ mean_ may - be. Be - Bop - a - Lu - la, she -

- e - 's_ my ba - by doll, my ba - by doll, my ba - by doll.

Additional Lyrics

2. Well, now she's the woman that's got that beat,
Oh, she's the woman with the flyin' feet.
Ah, she's the woman that walks around the store,
She's the woman that yells more, more, more, more.

Bye Bye Love

Words and Music by Felice Bryant and Boudleaux Bryant

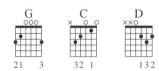

Intro
Moderately fast

Chorus

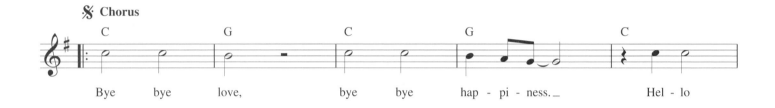

Bye bye love, bye bye hap - pi - ness. _ Hel - lo

lon - li - ness, _ I think I'm gon - na cry. ____ Bye bye

love, bye bye sweet ca - ress. _ Hel - lo emp - ti - ness, _ I

To Coda

feel like I could die. ____ Bye bye my love good - bye. 1. There goes my

Copyright © 1957 by HOUSE OF BRYANT PUBLICATIONS, Gatlinburg, TN
Copyright Renewed
All Foreign Rights Controlled by ACUFF-ROSE MUSIC, INC.
International Copyright Secured   All Rights Reserved

Verse

ba - by _____ with some - one new. _____ She sure looks

2. *See additional lyrics*

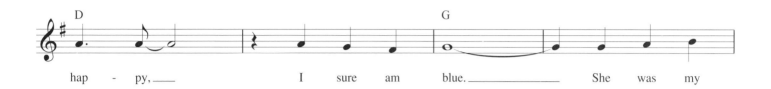

hap - py, _____ I sure am blue. _____ She was my

ba - by _____ till he stepped in. _____ Good - bye to

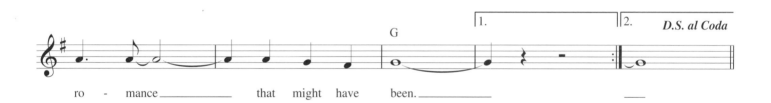

|1. |2.   *D.S. al Coda*

ro - mance _____ that might have been. _____ _____

✛ **Coda**

Outro   *Repeat and fade*

bye   my   love   good - bye.   Bye

Additional Lyrics

2. I'm through with romance, I'm through with love.
    I'm through with counting the stars above.
    And here's the reason that I'm so free;
    My lovin' baby is through with me.

Chantilly Lace

Words and Music by J.P. Richardson

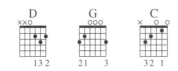

Intro
Moderately

Verse

Spoken: Hello, baby.   1. *Ya,*   *this is the Big Bopper speakin'.*
2., 3. *See additional lyrics*

Ha, ha, ha, ha, ha, ha.   *Oh, you sweet thing!*

Do I what?   *Will I what?*

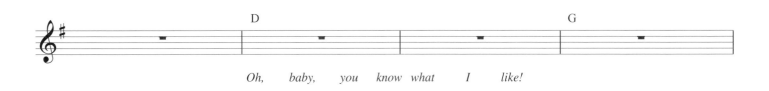

Oh, baby, you know what I like!

Chorus

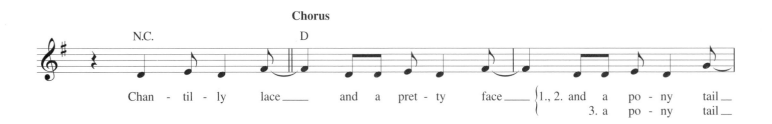

Chan - til - ly lace____ and a pret - ty face____ {1., 2. and a po - ny tail____
3. a po - ny tail____

Copyright © 1958 by Fort Knox Music Inc., Trio Music Company, Inc. and Glad Music Co.
Copyright Renewed
International Copyright Secured   All Rights Reserved
Used by Permission

a - hang - in' down,_____ a wig - gle in her walk and a gig - gle in her

1. talk.
2., 3. talk, Lord.

1., 3. Make the world go 'round._____ 1. There ain't
2. Make the world go 'round,__ round, round.__ 2., 3. There ain't a

noth - in' in the world | like a big eyed girl__ to make me act so fun - ny, make me
noth - in' in the world |

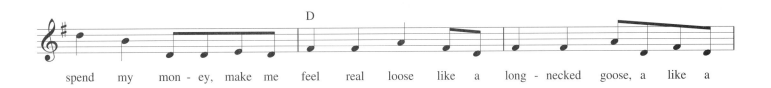

spend my mon - ey, make me feel real loose like a long - necked goose, a like a

| 1., 2. | 3. |

girl. *Spoken: Oh, baby, that's a what I like!*   girl. *Shouted: Oh, baby, that's a what I like!*

Additional Lyrics

2. *Spoken:* What's that, baby?
But, but, but,
Oh, honey,
But, oh baby, you know what I like!

3. *Spoken:* What's that, honey?
Pick you up at eight, and don't be late?
But, baby, I ain't got no money, honey!
Ha, ha, ha, ha, ha.
Oh, alright, honey, you know what I like!

Do Wah Diddy Diddy

Words and Music by Jeff Barry and Ellie Greenwich

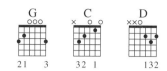

Intro

Moderate Rock

Verse

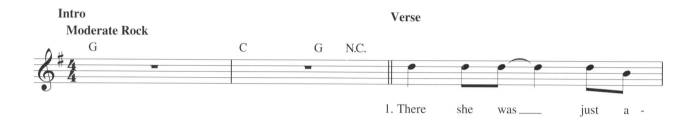

1. There she was ___ just a-

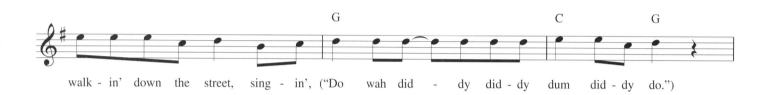

walk-in' down the street, sing-in', ("Do wah did - dy did-dy dum did-dy do.")

Snap-pin' her fin - gers and shuf-fl-in' ___ her feet, sing-in', ("Do wah did - dy did-dy

dum did-dy do.") She looked good. (Looked good.) She looked fine. (Looked fine.) She looked

good, she looked fine and I near-ly lost my mind. 2. Be - fore I knew ___ it she was

3. *See additional lyrics*

walk-in' next to me, sing-in', ("Do wah did - dy did-dy dum did-dy do.")

© 1963 (Renewed) TRIO MUSIC COMPANY, INC. and UNIVERSAL - SONGS OF POLYGRAM INTERNATIONAL, INC.
All Rights Reserved

Hold - in' my hand___ just as nat - u - ral as can be, sing - in', ("Do wah did - dy did - dy

dum did - dy do.") We walked on (Walked on.) to my door. (My door.) We walked

Bridge

on to my door, then we kissed a lit - tle more.

Whoa,_____ I knew we was fall - ing in love._____

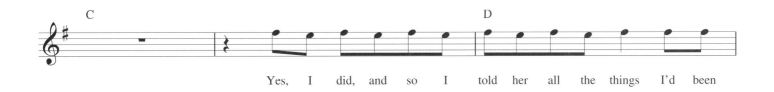

Yes, I did, and so I told her all the things I'd been

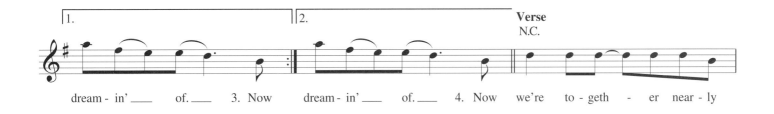

dream - in'___ of.___ 3. Now dream - in'___ of.___ 4. Now we're to - geth - er near - ly

Verse

ev - 'ry sin - gle day, sing - in', ("Do wah did - dy did - dy dum did - dy do.")

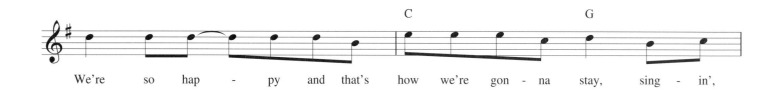

We're so hap - py and that's how we're gon - na stay, sing - in',

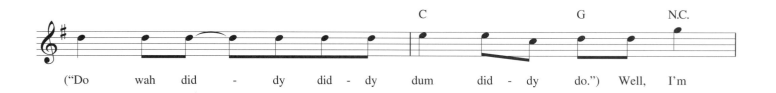

("Do wah did - dy did - dy dum did - dy do.") Well, I'm

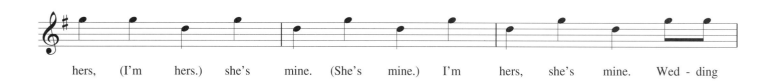

hers, (I'm hers.) she's mine. (She's mine.) I'm hers, she's mine. Wed - ding

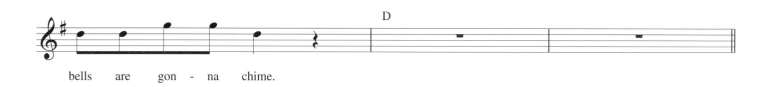

bells are gon - na chime.

Outro

("Do wah did - dy did - dy dum did - dy do. Do wah did - dy did - dy

dum did - dy do. Do wah did - dy did - dy dum did - dy do.")

Additional Lyrics

3. Now we're together nearly ev'ry single day, singin',
   ("Do wah diddy diddy dum diddy do.")
   We're so happy and that's how we're gonna stay, singin',
   ("Do wah diddy diddy dum diddy do.")
   Well, I'm hers, (I'm hers.)
   She's mine. (She's mine.)
   I'm hers, she's mine.
   Wedding bells are gonna chime.

Hound Dog

Words and Music by Jerry Leiber and Mike Stoller

Copyright © 1956 by Elvis Presley Music, Inc. and Lion Publishing Co., Inc.
Copyright Renewed, Assigned to Gladys Music and Universal - MCA Music Publishing, A Division of Universal Studios, Inc.
All Rights Administered by Cherry Lane Music Publishing Company, Inc. and Chrysalis Music
International Copyright Secured   All Rights Reserved

Donna

Words and Music by Ritchie Valens

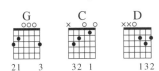

Intro

Moderate ballad

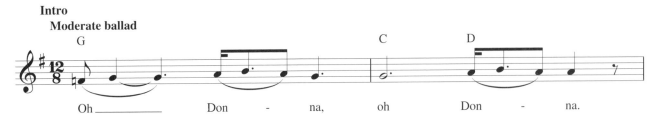

Oh _____ Don - na, oh Don - na.

Oh _____ Don - na, oh Don - na.

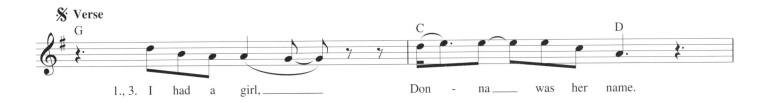

𝄋 Verse

1., 3. I had a girl, _____ Don - na _____ was her name.

Since she left me, _____ I've nev - er _____ been the same 'cause I

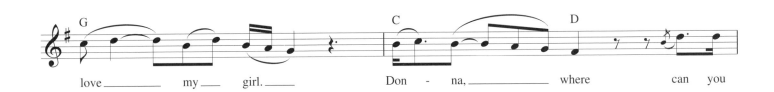

love _____ my _____ girl. Don - na, _____ where can you

To Coda ⊕

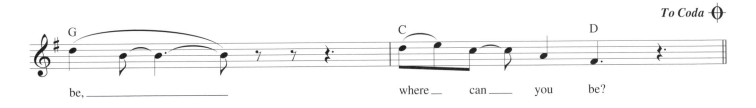

be, _____ where _____ can _____ you be?

Verse

2. Now _____ that you're gone, _____ I'm left _____ all _____ a - lone.

© 1958 (Renewed 1986) EMI LONGITUDE MUSIC
All Rights Reserved   International Copyright Secured   Used by Permission

All— by my - self_____ to won - der— and roam 'cause I

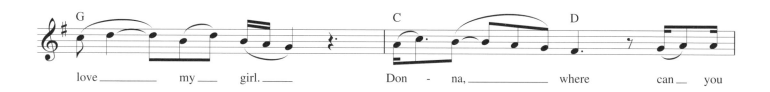

love_____ my— girl.____ Don - na,_____ where can you

be,_____ where_____ can you be? Oh well,

Bridge

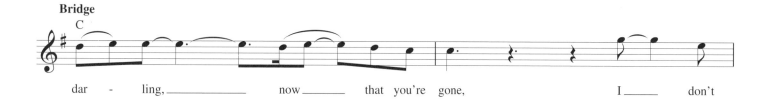

dar - ling,_____ now_____ that you're gone, I_____ don't

know what— I'll____ do. Oh,_____ time had— all my

D.S. al Coda

love for_____ you,_____ mm._____

Coda
Outro

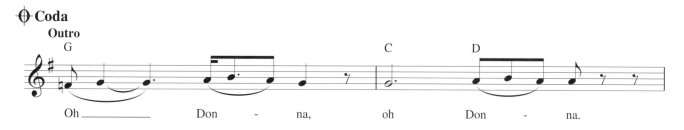

Oh_____ Don - na, oh Don - na.

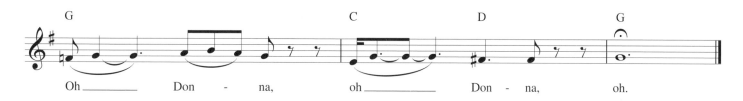

Oh_____ Don - na, oh Don - na, oh.

409

Words and Music by Brian Wilson, Gary Usher and Mike Love

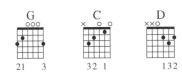

Intro
Moderately

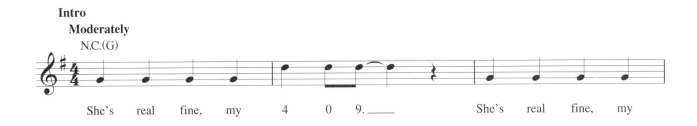

She's real fine, my 4 0 9. ___ She's real fine, my

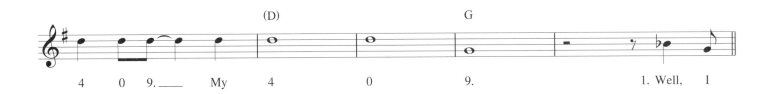

4 0 9. ___ My 4 0 9. 1. Well, I

Verse

saved my pen - nies, and I saved my dimes. ___ (Gid - dy - up, gid - dy - up
2. *See additional lyrics*

4 0 9.) ___ For I knew there would be a time. ___

(Gid - dy - up, gid - dy - up 4 0 9.) ___ When I would buy a brand ___

Copyright © 1962 IRVING MUSIC, INC.
Copyright Renewed
All Rights Reserved   Used by Permission

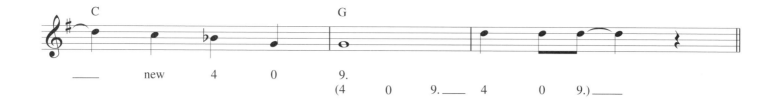

new 4 0 9.
(4 0 9. — 4 0 9.) —

Chorus

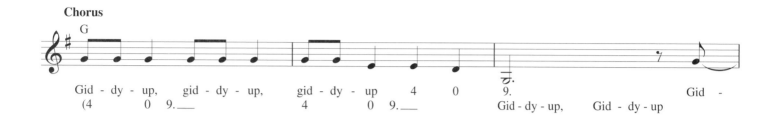

Gid - dy - up, gid - dy - up, gid - dy - up 4 0 9. Gid -
(4 0 9. — 4 0 9. — Gid - dy - up, Gid - dy - up

- dy - up 4 0 9. Gid - dy - up 4 0
4 0 9. — 4 0 9. — 4 0 9. —

9. Gid - dy - up 4 0...
Gid - dy - up, gid - dy - up 4 0 9.) —

Noth - ing can catch her, noth - ing can touch my 4 0 9. —

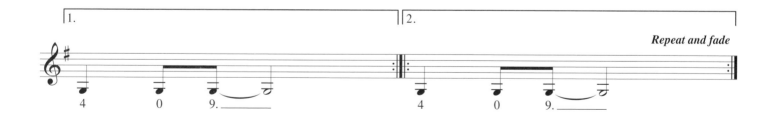

1. 4 0 9. —   2. *Repeat and fade* 4 0 9. —

Additional Lyrics

2. When I take her to the drag, she really shines.
(Giddy-up, giddy-up 409.)
She always turns in the fastest time.
(Giddy-up, giddy-up 409.)
My four-speed, dual-quad, posi-traction 409.
(409. 409.)

Get Back

Words and Music by John Lennon and Paul McCartney

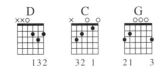

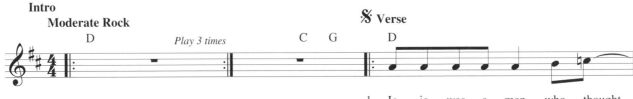

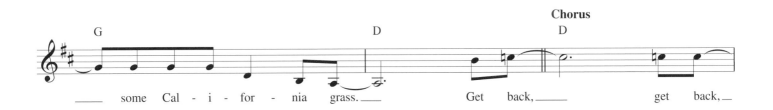

Copyright © 1969 Sony/ATV Songs LLC
Copyright Renewed
All Rights Administered by Sony/ATV Music Publishing, 8 Music Square West, Nashville, TN 37203
International Copyright Secured   All Rights Reserved

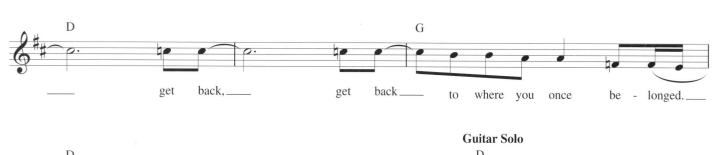

get back, _____ get back _____ to where you once be - longed. _____

Guitar Solo

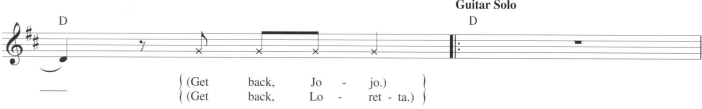

(Get back, Jo - jo.)
(Get back, Lo - ret - ta.)

1.

2. **Chorus**

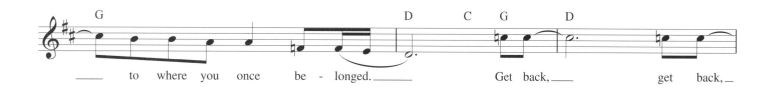

Get back, _____ get back, _____ get back _____

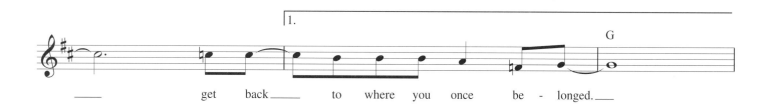

_____ to where you once be - longed. _____ Get back, _____ get back, _____

1.

_____ get back _____ to where you once be - longed. _____

2. *D.S. and fade*

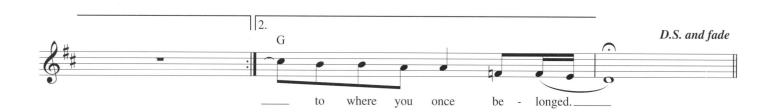

_____ to where you once be - longed. _____

Additional Lyrics

2. Sweet Loretta Martin thought she was a woman,
But she was another man.
All the girls around her say she's got it comin',
But she gets it while she can.

Give Me One Reason

Words and Music by Tracy Chapman

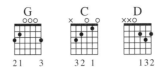

Intro
Moderately

Verse

1. Give me one rea-son to stay here ___ and I'll turn right back a - round. ___

Give me one rea-son to stay here ___ and I'll turn right back a -

round. ___ Said I don't wan-na leave you lone - ly, ___

you ___ got to make me change my mind. ___

© 1996 EMI APRIL MUSIC INC. and PURPLE RABBIT MUSIC
All Rights Controlled and Administered by EMI APRIL MUSIC INC.
All Rights Reserved   International Copyright Secured   Used by Permission

Additional Lyrics

3. Give me one reason to stay here
   And I'll turn right back around.
   (You can see the turn in me.)
   Give me one reason to stay here
   And I'll turn right back around.
   (You can see the turn in me.)
   Said I don't wanna leave you lonely,
   You got to make me change my mind.

6. This youthful heart can love you,
   Yes, and give you what you need.
   I said this youthful heart can love you,
   Ho, and give you what you need.
   But I'm too old to go chasin' you around,
   Wastin' my precious energy.

4. I don't want no one to squeeze me,
   They might take away my life.
   I don't want no one to squeeze me,
   They might take away my life.
   I just want someone to hold me,
   Oh, and rock me through the night.

7. Give me one reason to stay here,
   Yes, now turn right back around.
   (Around. You can see the turn in me.)
   Give me one reason to stay here
   Oh, I'll turn right back around.
   (You can see the turn in me.)
   Said I don't wanna leave you lonely,
   You got to make me change my mind.

8. Baby, just give me one reason,
   Oh, give me just one reason why.
   Baby, just give me one reason,
   Oh, give me just one reason why, I should stay.
   Said I told you that I loved you,
   And there ain't no more to say.

Gloria

Words and Music by Van Morrison

Copyright © 1965 by January Music Corp. and Hyde Park Music Company Ltd.
Copyright Renewed
Published in the U.S.A. and Canada by Unichappell Music Inc. and Bernice Music, Inc.
All Rights Administered by Unichappell Music Inc.
International Copyright Secured   All Rights Reserved

Additional Lyrics

2. She comes around here, just about midnight.
   She make me feel so good, Lord, I wanna say she make me feel alright.
   She comes walkin' down my street; a well, she comes to my house.
   She knock upon my door, and then she comes to my room.
   Then she make me feel alright.

Great Balls of Fire

Words and Music by Otis Blackwell and Jack Hammer

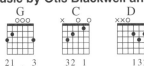

Verse

Bright Rock

1. You shake my nerves and you rat-tle my brain.

Too much love drives a man in-sane. You broke my will,

but what a thrill. Good-ness gra-cious, great___ balls of fire!

I laughed at love 'cause I thought it was fun-ny.

You came a-long and you moved___ me, hon-ey. I changed my mind,

love's just fine. ___ Good-ness gra-cious, great___ balls of fire!

% **Bridge**

Kiss me, ba-by. Woo, ___ it feels good.

Hold me, ba-by. Well, I want to love you like a

Copyright © 1957 by Chappell & Co. and Unichappell Music Inc.
Copyright Renewed
International Copyright Secured   All Rights Reserved

lov - er should.___ You're fine,___ so kind,___

got to tell this world that you're mine, mine, mine, mine.___

Verse

2., 3. I chew my nails and I twid - dle my thumb.___ I'm real ner - vous but it

To Coda ⊕

sure is fun.___ Come on, ba - by, you're driv - ing me cra - zy.

Piano Solo

Good - ness gra - cious, great___ balls of fire!

D.S. al Coda

Well,___

⊕ **Coda**

Good - ness gra - cious, great___ balls of fire!

Hang on Sloopy

Words and Music by Wes Farrell and Bert Russell

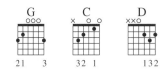

Chorus

Moderate Rock

Hang on Sloo-py, Sloo-py hang on. ___

Verse

1. Sloo-py lives ___ in a ver-y bad ___ part of town. ___
2., 3. *See additional lyrics*

And ev-'ry-bod-y, yeah, ___ tries to put my Sloo-py

1.
down. ___

2.
And so I sing out:

Chorus

Hang on Sloo-py, Sloo-py hang on. ___

Hang on Sloo-py, Sloo-py hang on. ___

3.
Outro

Come on, ___ Sloo-py. (Come on, come on.) ___

Copyright © 1964, 1965 by Morris Music, Inc., Sony/ATV Songs LLC and Sloopy II, Inc. in the U.S.
Copyright Renewed
All Rights on behalf of Sony/ATV Songs LLC Administered by Sony/ATV Music Publishing, 8 Music Square West, Nashville, TN 37203
All Rights outside the U.S. Administered by Morris Music, Inc.
International Copyright Secured   All Rights Reserved

Additional Lyrics

2. Sloopy, I don't care what your daddy do,
'Cause you know, Sloopy girl, I'm in love with you.

3. Sloopy, let your hair down, let it hang down on me.
Sloopy, let your hair down, girl, let it hang down on me.

Hanky Panky

Words and Music by Jeff Barry and Ellie Greenwich

Chorus

Moderately

My ba - by does ____ the hank - y pank - y, yeah, my ba - by does ____

____ the hank - y pank - y. My ba - by does ____ the hank - y pank - y,

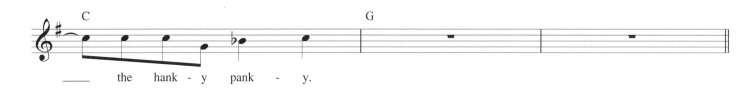

my ba - by does ____ the hank - y pank - y. Hey, my ba - by does ____

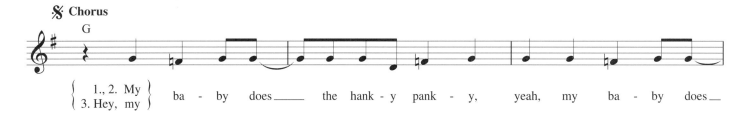

____ the hank - y pank - y.

𝄋 Chorus

{ 1., 2. My } { 3. Hey, my } ba - by does ____ the hank - y pank - y, yeah, my ba - by does ____

____ the hank - y pank - y. { 1. Hey, my } { 2., 3. My } ba - by does ____ the hank - y pank - y,

my ba - by does ____ the hank - y pank - y. { 1. Hey, my } { 2., 3. My } ba - by does ____

Copyright © 1962 by Alley Music Corp. and Trio Music Company, Inc.
Copyright Renewed
International Copyright Secured   All Rights Reserved
Used by Permission

I Fought the Law

Words and Music by Sonny Curtis

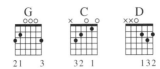

Intro

Driving Rock

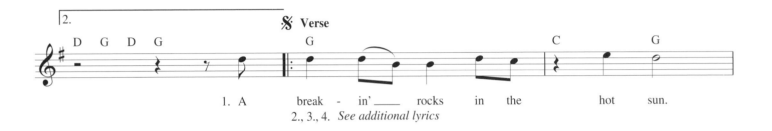

1. A break - in' rocks in the hot sun.
2., 3., 4. *See additional lyrics*

I fought the law ___ and the law won.

I fought the law ___ and the law ___ won.

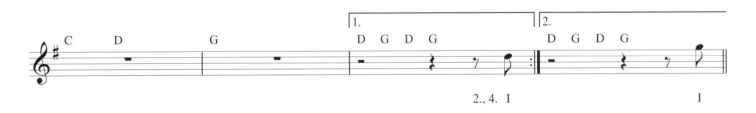

2., 4. I   I

Bridge

left my ba - by and I feel so bad. ___   I

Copyright © 1961 (Renewed 1990) by Acuff-Rose Music, Inc.
All Rights Reserved   Used by Permission

guess   my   race   is   run. _____   Well, she's   the   best ___ girl

I've   ev - er   had. _____   I   fought   the   law ___ and   the

law   won.   I   fought   the   law ___ and   the

law _   won.

Guitar Solo

Coda

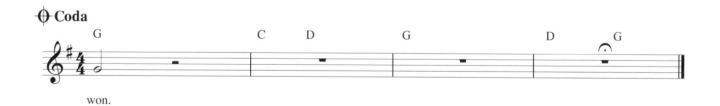

won.

Additional Lyrics

2., 4.   I miss my baby and the good fun.
         I fought the law and the law won.
         I fought the law and the law won.

3.   Robbin' people with a six gun.
      I fought the law and the law won.
      I fought the law and the law won.

Kansas City

Words and Music by Jerry Leiber and Mike Stoller

Intro

Moderate Blues

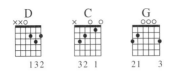

I'm go - in' to

Chorus

Kan - sas Cit - y,   Kan - sas Cit - y here I come.   I'm go - in' to

Kan - sas Cit - y,   Kan - sas Cit - y here I come.   They got a

cra - zy way of lov - in' there and I'm gon - na   get me some. ___

Verse

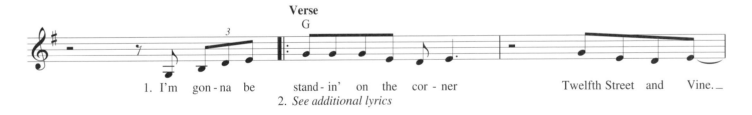

1. I'm gon - na be   stand - in' on the cor - ner   Twelfth Street and Vine. ___

2. *See additional lyrics*

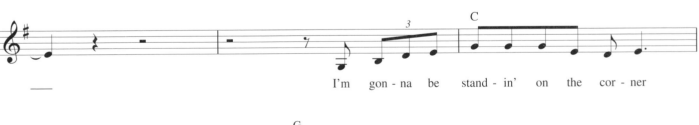

___   I'm gon - na be stand - in' on the cor - ner

Twelfth Street and Vine ___   with my

© 1952 (Renewed) JERRY LEIBER MUSIC, MIKE STOLLER MUSIC and NANCY NATHAN GOLDSTEIN
All Rights Reserved

Additional Lyrics

2. I'm goin' to pack my clothes, leave at the crack of dawn.
   I'm goin' to pack my clothes, leave at the crack of dawn.
   My old lady will be sleepin' and she won't know where I've gone.

La Bamba

By Ritchie Valens

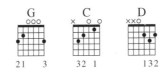

Intro
Moderately fast

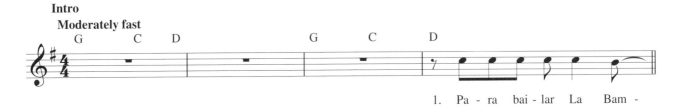

1. Pa - ra bai - lar La Bam -

% Verse

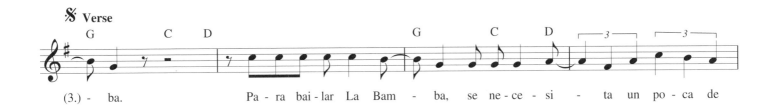

(3.) - ba. Pa - ra bai - lar La Bam - ba, se ne - ce - si - ta un po - ca de

gra - cia. _ Un - a po - ca de gra - cia pa'ra mi pa'ra ti _ y ar - ri - ba, ar - ri -

To Coda ⊕

- ba, y ar - ri - ba, ar - ri - ba, por ti se re, _ por ti se

re, por ti se re. Yo no soy mar - i - ne - ro. Yo no soy mar - i -

ne - ro, soy cap - i - tan, _ soy cap - i - tan, _ soy cap - i - tan.

© 1958 (Renewed 1986) EMI LONGITUDE MUSIC and WARNER-TAMERLANE PUBLISHING CORP.
All Rights for the United States Controlled and Administered by EMI LONGITUDE MUSIC
All Rights Reserved International Copyright Secured Used by Permission

Chorus

Bam - ba, bam - ba.   Bam - ba, bam - ba.   Bam - ba, bam -

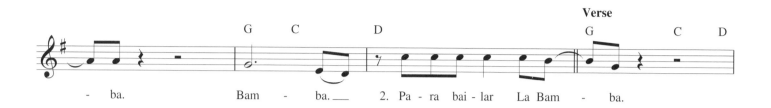

Verse

- ba.   Bam - ba.___   2. Pa - ra bai - lar   La Bam - ba.

Pa - ra bai - lar   La Bam - ba,   se ne - ce - si - ta un po - ca de

gra - cia.   Un - a po - ca de   gra - cia pa'ra mi pa'ra ti___

Guitar Solo

Play 7 times

___ y ar - ri - ba, ar - ri - ba.

D.S. al Coda   **Coda**

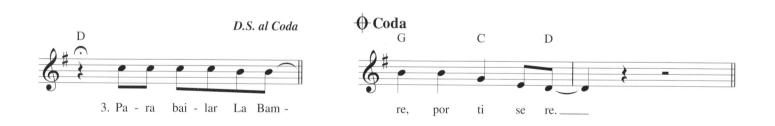

3. Pa - ra   bai - lar   La Bam -   re,   por   ti   se   re.___

Outro-Chorus   *Repeat and fade*

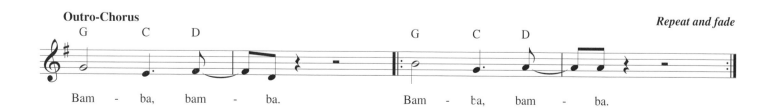

Bam - ba, bam - ba.   Bam - ba, bam - ba.

Lay Down Sally

Words and Music by Eric Clapton, Marcy Levy and George Terry

Copyright © 1977 by Eric Patrick Clapton and Throat Music Ltd.
All Rights for the U.S. Administered by Unichappell Music Inc.
International Copyright Secured   All Rights Reserved

Lively Up Yourself

Words and Music by Bob Marley

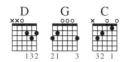

Copyright © 1975 Fifty-Six Hope Road Music, Ltd., Odnil Music, Ltd. and Blue Mountain Music, Ltd.
All Rights for North and South America Controlled and Administered by Rykomusic, Inc.
All Rights for the rest of the world Controlled and Administered by Rykomusic, Ltd.
International Copyright Secured   All Rights Reserved

To Coda ⊕

Chorus

Long Tall Sally

Words and Music by Enotris Johnson, Richard Penniman and Robert Blackwell

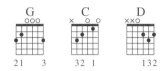

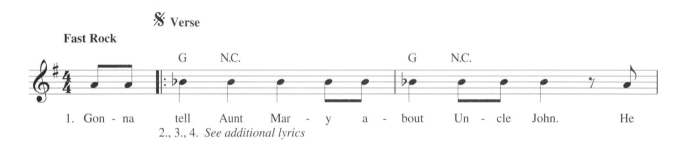

% Verse

Fast Rock

1. Gon - na tell Aunt Mar - y a - bout Un - cle John. He
2., 3., 4. *See additional lyrics*

claims he has the mis - 'ry, but he has a lot of fun. Oh, ba -

- by, yes, ___ ba - by. Woo, ___ ba -

4th time, To Coda ⊕

- by, ___ hav - in' me some ___ fun to - night. ___ Yeah. ___

1. **2.** **Saxophone Solo**

2., 4. Well, ___ Ow! ___

Copyright © 1956 Sony/ATV Songs LLC
Copyright Renewed
All Rights Administered by Sony/ATV Music Publishing, 8 Music Square West, Nashville, TN 37203
International Copyright Secured   All Rights Reserved

Additional Lyrics

2., 4. Well, long tall Sally she's built pretty sweet.
   She's got ev'rything that Uncle John need.
   Oh, baby, yes, baby.
   Woo, baby, havin' me some fun tonight. Yeah.

3. Well, I saw Uncle John with blonde headed Sally.
   He saw Aunt Mary comin' and he ducked back in the alley.
   Oh, baby, yes, baby.
   Woo, baby, havin' me some fun tonight. Yeah. Ow!

Love Me Do

Words and Music by John Lennon and Paul McCartney

Intro
Moderately fast

1.-4. Love, love me do, _____ you know I love you. _____ I'll al - ways be true, _____ so _____ please _____

_____ love me do. _____ Whoa, _ love _____ me do. _____

Bridge

Some - one to love, some - bod - y new. _____ Some - one to love, some - one like _ you.

© 1962, 1963 MPL COMMUNICATIONS LTD.
© Renewed 1990, 1991 MPL COMMUNICATIONS LTD. and LENONO.MUSIC
All Rights for MPL COMMUNICATIONS LTD. in the U.S. and Canada Controlled and Administered by BEECHWOOD MUSIC CORP.
All Renewal Rights for LENONO.MUSIC in the U.S. Controlled and Administered by EMI BLACKWOOD MUSIC INC.
All Rights Reserved   International Copyright Secured   Used by Permission

Harmonica Solo

D.S. al Coda 2

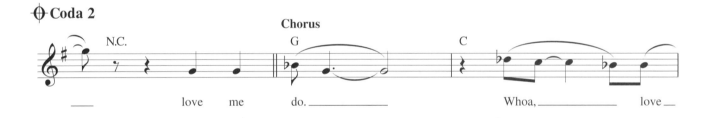

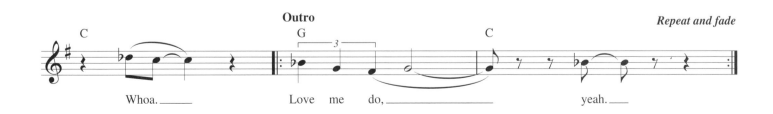

Mellow Yellow

Words and Music by Donovan Leitch

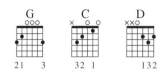

1. I'm just mad a - bout Saf - fron, Saf - fron's mad a - bout me.
2., 3., 5., 6. *See additional lyrics*
4. *Instrumental*

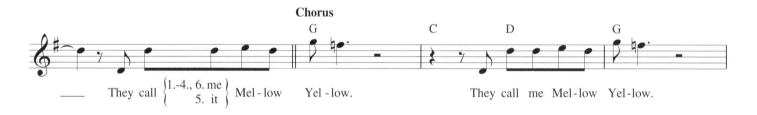

I'm just mad a - bout Saf - fron, she's just mad a - bout me.

Chorus

They call {1.-4., 6. me / 5. it} Mel - low Yel - low. They call me Mel - low Yel - low.

1.-5.

They call me Mel - low Yel - low.

6. Outro   *Repeat and fade*

Yel - low.   They call me Mel - low

Additional Lyrics

2. I'm just mad about Fourteen,
   Fourteen's mad about me.
   I'm just mad about Fourteen,
   She's just mad about me.

3. Born high, forever to fly,
   Wind velocity: nil.
   Born high, forever to fly,
   If you want your cup I will fill.

5. Electrical banana
   Is going to be a sudden craze.
   Electrical banana
   Is bound to be the very next phase.

6. I'm just mad about Saffron;
   I'm just mad about her.
   I'm just mad about Saffron;
   She's just mad about me.

Copyright © 1966 by Donovan (Music) Ltd.
Copyright Renewed
All Rights Administered by Peer International Corporation
International Copyright Secured   All Rights Reserved

Move It on Over

Words and Music by Hank Williams

Additional Lyrics

2. She's changed the lock on our front door
   And my door key don't fit no more.
      So get it on over. (Move it on over.) Scoot it on over. (Move it on over.)
      Move over, skinny dog, 'cause the fat dog's movin' in.

3. This dog house here is mighty small
   But it's better than no house at all.
      So ease it on over. (Move it on over.) Drag it on over. (Move it on over.)
      Move over, old dog, 'cause a new dog's movin' in.

4. She told me not to play around,
   But I done let the deal go down.
      So pack it on over. (Move it on over.) Tote it on over. (Move it on over.)
      Move over, nice dog, 'cause a mad dog's movin' in.

5. She warned me once, she warned me twice,
   But I don't take no one's advice.
      So scratch it on over. (Move it on over.) Shake it on over. (Move it on over.)
      Move over, short dog, 'cause a tall dog's movin' in.

6. She'll crawl back to me on her knees.
   I'll be busy scratchin' fleas.
      So slide it on over. (Move it on over.) Sneak it on over. (Move it on over.)
      Move over, good dog, 'cause a mad dog's movin' in.

7. Remember pup, before you whine,
   That side's yours and this side's mine.
      So shove it on over. (Move it on over.) Sweep it on over. (Move it on over.)
      Move over, cold dog, 'cause a hot dog's movin' in.

Copyright © 1947 (Renewed 1974) by Acuff-Rose Music, Inc. and Hiriam Music in the U.S.A.
All Rights for Hiriam Music Administered by Rightsong Music Inc.
All Rights outside the U.S.A. Controlled by Acuff-Rose Music, Inc.
All Rights Reserved   Used by Permission

Mony, Mony

Words and Music by Bobby Bloom, Tommy James, Ritchie Cordell and Bo Gentry

© 1968 (Renewed 1996) EMI LONGITUDE MUSIC
All Rights Reserved   International Copyright Secured   Used by Permission

come on, ___   al - right, ba - by.   Say yeah, ___   yeah, __

so good,   al - right. ___   I say yeah, ___

Mo - ny, Mo - ny.   Mo - ny, Mo - ny.   Mo - ny, Mo - ny.)   (Yeah, __

D

1.
G

yeah, ___   yeah, __   yeah, ___   yeah. __   Come on.

yeah, __   yeah,   yeah,   yeah.)   ah! ___

Breakdown

2.
G   C   N.C.   *So good.*

(Ooh, __ I love ya   Mo - ny, Mo - Mo - Mo - ny.   Ooh, __ I love ya

So fine.

Mo - ny, Mo - Mo - Mo - ny.   Ooh, __ I love ya   Mo - ny, Mo - Mo - Mo -

Al - right.   C

Say   Mo - ny,   Mo - ny.   Yeah, __

- ny.   Ooh, __ I love ya   Mo - ny, Mo - ny.

D.S. and fade

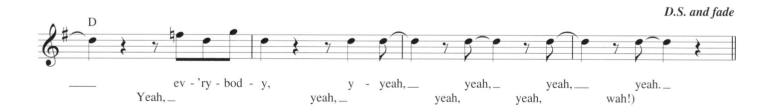

D

ev - 'ry - bod - y,   y - yeah, __   yeah, __   yeah, __   yeah. __

Yeah, __   yeah, __   yeah,   yeah,   wah!)

Additional Lyrics

2. Wake me, shake me, Mony, Mony.
    Shotgun, get it done. Come on, Mony.
    Don't 'cha stop cookin', it feels so good, yeah.
    Hey! Well, but don't stop now, hey,
    Come on Mony. Well, come on, Mony.

Not Fade Away

Words and Music by Charles Hardin and Norman Petty

Additional Lyrics

2. My love is bigger than a Cadillac.
   I try to show it and you drive me back.
   Your love for me got to be real,
   For you to know a just how I feel.
   A love for real'll not fade away.

3. I'm a gonna tell you how it's gonna be.
   You're gonna give a your love to me.
   A love to last more than one day.
   A love that's love'll not fade away.
   A love that's love'll not fade away.

© 1957 (Renewed) MPL COMMUNICATIONS, INC. and WREN MUSIC CO.
All Rights Reserved

Rain

Words and Music by John Lennon and Paul McCartney

Copyright © 1966 Sony/ATV Songs LLC
Copyright Renewed
All Rights Administered by Sony/ATV Music Publishing, 8 Music Square West, Nashville, TN 37203
International Copyright Secured   All Rights Reserved

Rock Around the Clock

Words and Music by Max C. Freedman and Jimmy DeKnight

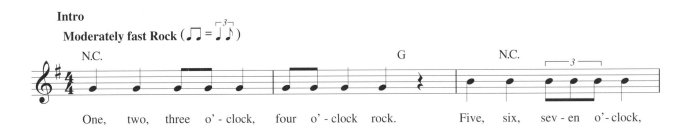

Intro

Moderately fast Rock

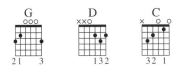

One, two, three o'-clock, four o'-clock rock. Five, six, sev-en o'-clock,

eight o'-clock rock. Nine, ten, e-lev-en o'-clock twelve o'-clock rock. We're gon-na

Verse

rock a-round the clock to-night.__ 1. Put your glad rags on,
2., 4., 5., 6. *See additional lyrics*
3. *Instrumental*

join me, hon.__ We'll have some fun when the clock strikes one. We're gon-na

rock a-round the clock to-night.__ We're gon-na rock, rock, rock till

Copyright © 1953 Myers Music Inc. and Capano Music
Copyright Renewed 1981
All Rights on behalf of Myers Music Inc. Administered by Sony/ATV Music Publishing, 8 Music Square West, Nashville TN 37203
International Copyright Secured   All Rights Reserved

broad   day - light. ___   We're gon - na   rock,   gon - na   rock   a -   round ___   the   clock ___   to - night. ___

___   2. When the

2. When the

6. When   the

_____

Additional Lyrics

2. When the clock strikes two, three and four,
    If the band slows down we'll yell for more.
    We're gonna rock around the clock tonight.
    We're gonna rock, rock, rock till broad daylight.
    We're gonna rock, gonna rock around the clock tonight.

4. When the chimes ring five, six and seven,
    We'll be right in seventh heaven.
    We're gonna rock around the clock tonight.
    We're gonna rock, rock, rock till broad daylight.
    We're gonna rock, gonna rock around the clock tonight.

5. When it' eight, nine, ten, eleven too,
    I'll be goin' strong and so will you.
    We're gonna rock around the clock tonight.
    We're gonna rock, rock, rock till broad daylight.
    We're gonna rock, gonna rock around the clock tonight.

6. When the clock strikes twelve, we'll cool off then,
    Start a rockin' 'round the clock again.
    We're gonna rock around the clock tonight.
    We're gonna rock, rock, rock till broad daylight.
    We're gonna rock, gonna rock around the clock tonight.

Rock This Town

Words and Music by Brian Setzer

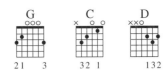

Moderately fast

% **Verse**

1. Well, my ba - by and me ___ went out ___ late Sat - ur - day night. ___
2., 3. *See additional lyrics*

I had my hair piled high, my

ba - by just looked ___ so right. ___ Well, ___

pick you up at ten, gon - na get you home at two. Your ma - ma don't know what I

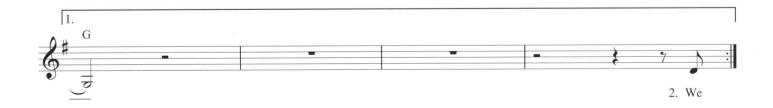

got in store for you. But, ba - by, that's all right, ___ we're look - in' as cool as can be. ___

1.

G

2. We

© 1981 EMI LONGITUDE MUSIC and ROCKIN' BONES MUSIC
All Rights Controlled and Administered by EMI LONGITUDE MUSIC
All Rights Reserved   International Copyright Secured   Used by Permission

Chorus

We're gon-na rock this town, rock it in-side out.

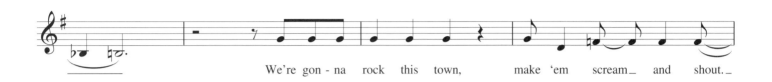

We're gon-na rock this town, make 'em scream and shout.

Well, let's rock, rock, rock, man, rock.
Well, let's rock, rock, rock, rock.

Rock till we pop, we're gon-na roll till we drop. We're gon-na rock this town, rock
Rock till we pop, we're gon-na roll till we drop. Rock this town, rip

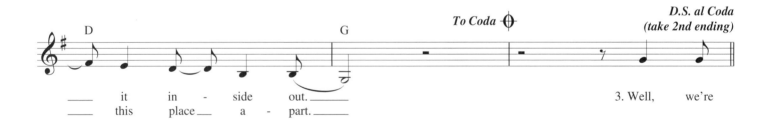

it in-side out.
this place a-part.

3. Well, we're

Coda

Outro-Chorus

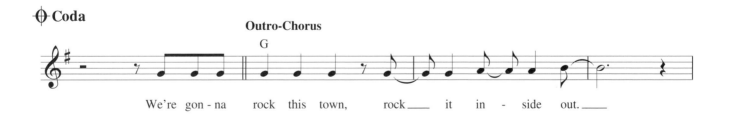

We're gon-na rock this town, rock it in-side out.

We're gon-na rock this town, make 'em scream and shout.

Well, let's rock, rock,___ rock,___ rock.___ Rock till we pop, we're gon - na

roll till we drop. We're gon - na rock this town, rock___ it in - side out.___

We're gon - na rock this town, rock___ it in - side out.___

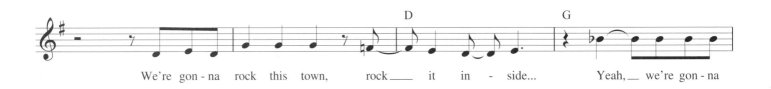

We're gon - na rock this town, rock___ it in - side... Yeah,___ we're gon - na

rock this town,___ tear___ it up,___ we're gon - na rip it down.___ Rock___

___ this town,___ rock___ it in - side out._____

Additional Lyrics

2. We found a little place that really didn't look half bad.
    I had a whiskey on the rocks and change of a dollar for the jukebox.
    Well, I put a quarter right into that can,
    But all it played was disco, man.
    Come on, pretty baby, let's get out of here right away.

3. Well, we're havin' a ball just tearing up the big dance floor.
    Well, there's a real square cat; he looks nineteen-seventy-four.
    Well, he looked at me once, he looked at me twice.
    Look at me again and there's gonna be a fight.
    We're gonna rock this town, rip this place apart.

See See Rider

Adapted and Arranged by Elvis Presley

Additional Lyrics

2., 4. { Oh, well, I'm }
      { Well, I'm } going away baby,
And I won't be back 'til Fall.
Well, I'm going, going, going, going away, baby,
And I won't be back 'til Fall.
If I find me a good girl,
I won't, I won't, I won't a be back at all.
What'd I say, now.

Copyright © 1970 by Elvis Presley Music, Inc.
Copyright Renewed and Assigned to Elvis Presley Music
All Rights Administered by Cherry River Music Co. and Chrysalis Songs
International Copyright Secured   All Rights Reserved

Rockin' Robin

Words and Music by J. Thomas

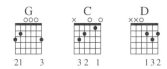

Intro
Bright shuffle

Twee - dle - e dee - dle - e - dee, twee - dle - e dee - dle - e - dee.

Tweet, tweet, tweet, tweet. 1. He (3.) rocks in the tree - top all __
2. *See additional lyrics*

__ the day long, hop - pin' and a bop - pin' and a

sing - in' his song. All the lit - tle birds on Jay - bird Street __ love __

__ to hear the rob - in go - in' tweet, tweet, tweet. Rock - in'

Chorus

rob - in, rock, rock, __ rock - in' rob - in.

Copyright © 2002 by HAL LEONARD CORPORATION
International Copyright Secured   All Rights Reserved

Blow, rock - in' rob - in 'cause we're real - ly gon - na rock to - night.___

Bridge

pret - ty lit - tle ra - ven at the bird band - stand taught___

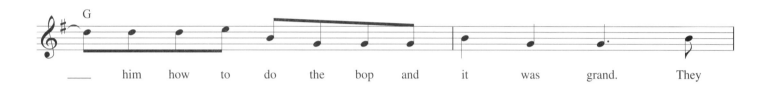

___ him how to do the bop and it was grand. They

start - ed go - in' stead - y and bless my soul, he

out - bopped the buz - zard and the or - i - ole. 3. He

⊕ Coda   **Outro**

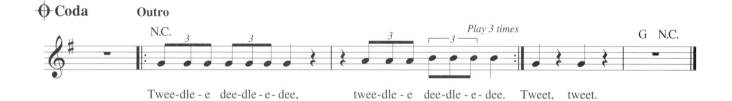

Twee-dle - e dee-dle - e- dee,   twee-dle - e dee-dle - e- dee.   Tweet,   tweet.

Additional Lyrics

2. Ev'ry little swallow, ev'ry chickadee,
   Ev'ry little bird in the tall oak tree.
   The wise old owl, the big black crow,
   Flap their wings singin' go, bird, go.

Save the Last Dance for Me

Words and Music by Doc Pomus and Mort Shuman

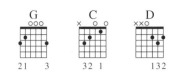

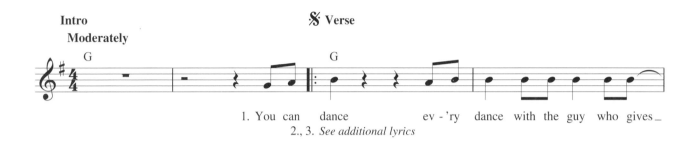

Intro
Moderately

𝄋 Verse

1. You can dance ev-'ry dance with the guy who gives
2., 3. *See additional lyrics*

____ you the eye; let him hold you tight. ____ You can

smile ____ ev-'ry smile for the man who held ____ your hand ____ 'neath the

Chorus

pale moon-light. ____ { 1., 2. But / 3. 'Cause } don't for - get who's tak - ing you home ____

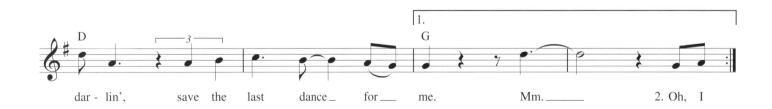

____ and in whose arms you're gon - na be. So dar - lin', save the last dance ____ for ____ me. Mm. ____ 2. Oh, I

Copyright © 1960 by Unichappell Music Inc.
Copyright Renewed
International Copyright Secured   All Rights Reserved

me.   Mm.   1. Ba - by, don't you know I   love you   so?____

2. *Instrumental*

Can't you feel it when we touch?   I will nev - er, nev - er

let us go.____   I love you, oh, so____ much.   3. You can

'Cause don't for - get who's tak - ing you home____ and in whose arms you're

gon-na be.   So, dar - lin', save the last dance__ for__ me.   Mm.____

Save   the last dance__ for__ me.   Mm - hh.____

Additional Lyrics

2. Oh, I know that the music's fine
   Like sparkling wine; go and have your fun.
   Laugh and sing, but while we're apart
   Don't give your heart to anyone.

3. You can dance, go and carry on
   Till the night is gone and it's time to go.
   If he asks if you're all alone,
   Can he take you home, you must tell him no.

See You Later, Alligator

Words and Music by Robert Guidry

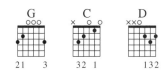

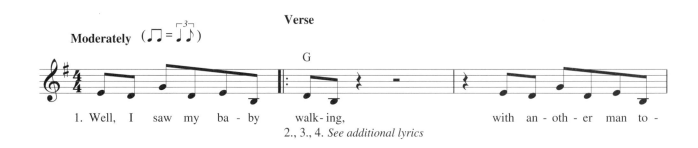

1. Well, I saw my ba-by walk-ing, with an-oth-er man to-

2., 3., 4. *See additional lyrics*

day. __ Well, I saw my ba-by walk-ing,

with an-oth-er man to-day. __ When I asked her what's the

mat-ter, this is what I heard her say.

Chorus

See you lat-er, al-li-ga-tor, af-ter 'while, croc-o-

Copyright © 1955, 1956 (Renewed) by Arc Music Corporation (BMI)
International Copyright Secured   All Rights Reserved
Used by Permission

dile. ___   See   you   lat - er,   al - li - ga - tor,

af - ter   'while,   croc - o - dile. ___   Can't   you   see   you're   in   my

|1., 2., 3.

way,   now,   don't   you   know   you   cramp   my   style?

|4.

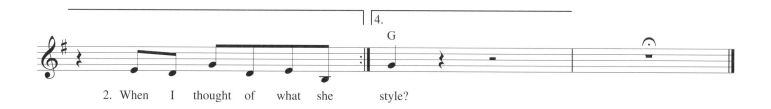

2. When   I   thought   of   what   she   style?

Additional Lyrics

2. When I thought of what she told me,
   Nearly made me lose my head.
   When I thought of what she told me,
   Nearly made me lose my head.
   But the next time that I saw her,
   Reminded her of what she said.

3. She said, I'm sorry, pretty daddy,
   You know my love is just for you.
   She said, I'm sorry, pretty daddy,
   You know my love is just for you.
   Won't you say that you'll forgive me,
   And say your love for me is true.

4. I said, wait a minute, 'gator,
   I know you meant it just for play.
   I said, wait a minute, 'gator,
   I know you meant it just for play.
   Don't you know you really hurt me,
   And this is what I have to say.

Shake, Rattle and Roll

Words and Music by Charles Calhoun

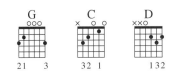

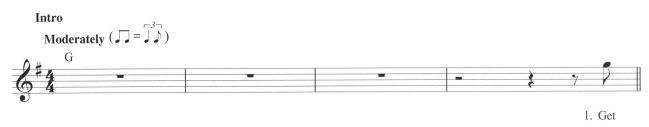

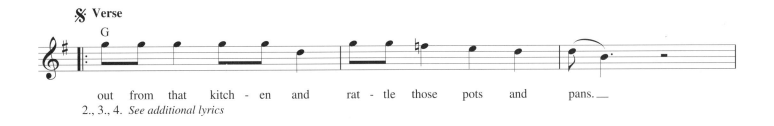

out from that kitch-en and rat-tle those pots and pans.___
2., 3., 4. See additional lyrics

Get out from that kitch-en and rat-tle those pots and pans.___

Well, roll my break-fast, 'cause I'm a hun-gry___ man.

I said shake, rat-tle and roll.____ I said

shake, rat-tle and roll.____ I said shake, rat-tle and roll.___

Copyright © 1954 by Unichappell Music Inc.
Copyright Renewed
International Copyright Secured   All Rights Reserved

I said shake, rat - tle and roll._____ Well, you

To Coda 2

nev - er do noth - in' to save your dog - gone_____ soul.__

Saxophone Solo

Shouted: Go!

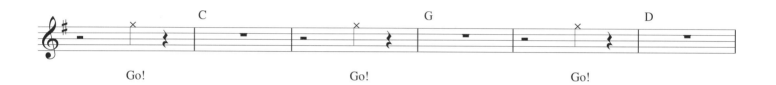

Go!   Go!   Go!

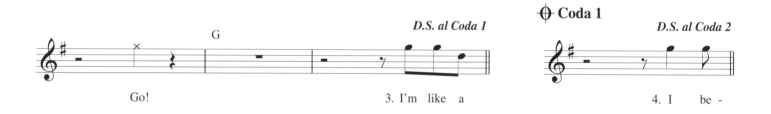

D.S. al Coda 1   **Coda 1**   *D.S. al Coda 2*

Go!   3. I'm like a   4. I be -

Coda 2

Shake,   rat - tle and roll._____

Additional Lyrics

2. Wearin' those dresses, your hair done up so nice.
   Wearin' those dresses, your hair done up so nice.
   You look so warm, but your heart is cold as ice.

3. I'm like a one-eyed cat, peepin' in a seafood store.
   I'm like a one-eyed cat, peepin' in a seafood store.
   I can look at you, tell you don't love me no more.

4. I believe you're doin' me wrong and now I know.
   I believe you're doin' me wrong and now I know.
   The more I work, the faster my money goes.

Stir It Up

Words and Music by Bob Marley

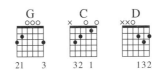

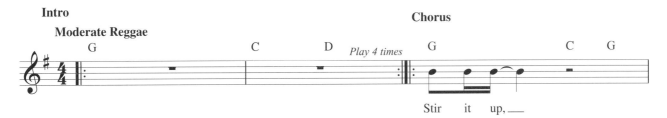

Intro

Moderate Reggae

Chorus

Stir it up, ___

lit - tle dar - ling, stir it up. ___ Come on and

stir it up, ___ lit - tle dar - ling, stir it up. ___

%Verse

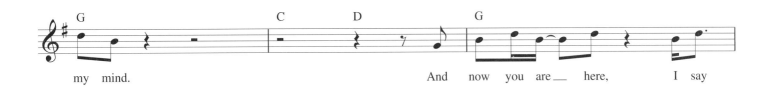

1. It's been a long, long time ___ since I've got you on

2., 3. *See additional lyrics*

my mind. And now you are ___ here, I say

it's so clear. ___ See what we can do, hon - ey, just me and you. Come on and

Copyright © 1972 Fifty-Six Hope Road Music, Ltd., Odnil Music, Ltd. and Blue Mountain Music, Ltd.
Copyright Renewed
All Rights for North and South America Controlled and Administered by Rykomusic, Inc.
All Rights for the rest of the world Controlled and Administered by Rykomusic, Ltd.
International Copyright Secured   All Rights Reserved

Additional Lyrics

2. I'll push the wood, I'll blaze your fire,
   Then I'll satisfy your, your heart's desire.
   Said I'll stir it, yeah, ev'ry minute, yeah.
   All you got to do, honey, is keep it in.

3. Oh, will you quench me while I'm thirsty?
   Or would you cool me down when I'm hot?
   Your recipe, darling, is so tasty,
   And you sure can stir your pot.

Stuck on You

Words and Music by Aaron Schroeder and J. Leslie McFarland

Copyright © 1960 by Gladys Music, Inc.
Copyright Renewed and Assigned to Gladys Music and Rachel's Own Music
All Rights for Gladys Music Administered by Cherry Lane Music Publishing Company, Inc. and Chrysalis Music
All Rights for Rachel's Own Music Administered by A. Schroeder International LLC
International Copyright Secured   All Rights Reserved

Additional Lyrics

2. I'm gonna squeeze my fingers through your long black hair,
   Squeeze you tighter than a grizzly bear.
   Uh, huh, huh. Yes siree, uh, huh.
   I'm gonna stick like glue.
   Stick because I'm stuck on you.

Surfin' U.S.A.

Words by Brian Wilson
Music by Chuck Berry

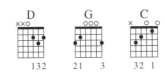

Bright Rock

Verse

1. If ev - 'ry - bod - y had an o - cean, ___
2. *See additional lyrics*

a - cross the U. S. A. ___ then ev - 'ry - bod - y'd be

surf - in' ___ like Cal - i - for - ni - a. ___

You'd see 'em wear - in' their bag - gies, ___ huar - a - chi san - dals too. ___

___ A bush - y, bush - y blonde hair - do, ___

surf - in' U. S. A. ___ You'll catch 'em surf - in' at

Copyright © 1958, 1963 (Renewed) by Arc Music Corporation (BMI) and Isalee Music Inc. (BMI)
International Copyright Secured   All Rights Reserved
Used by Permission

%D

Del Mar, ___ Ven - tu - ra Coun - ty line, ___

3. *Instrumental*

San - ta Cruz and Tres - sels, ___ Aus - tra - lia's Nar - a - bine, ___

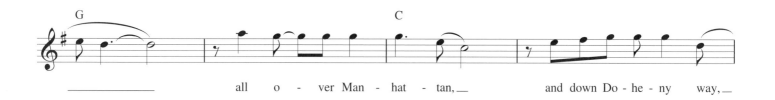

_____ all o - ver Man - hat - tan, ___ and down Do - he - ny way, ___

_____ ev - 'ry - bod - y's gone surf - in', ___ surf - in' U. S. A. ___

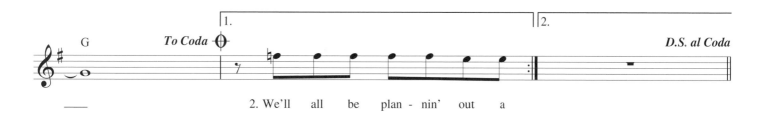

To Coda ⊕   *D.S. al Coda*

2. We'll all be plan - nin' out a

⊕ **Coda**

Outro   *Repeat and fade*

Ev - 'ry - bod - y's gone surf - in', ___ surf - in' U. S. A. ___

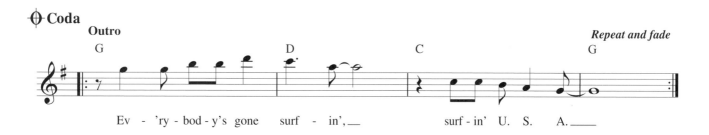

Additional Lyrics

2. We'll all be plannin' out a route, we're gonna take real soon.
We're waxin' down our surfboards, we can't wait for June.
We'll all be gone for the summer, we're on safari to stay.
Tell the teacher we're surfin', surfin' U.S.A.
At Haggarty's and Swami's, Pacific Palisades,
San Onofre and Sunset, Redondo Beach, L.A.,
All over La Jolla, at Waiamea Bay,
Ev'rybody's gone surfin', surfin' U.S.A.

Sweet Home Chicago

Words and Music by Robert Johnson

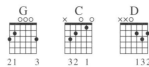

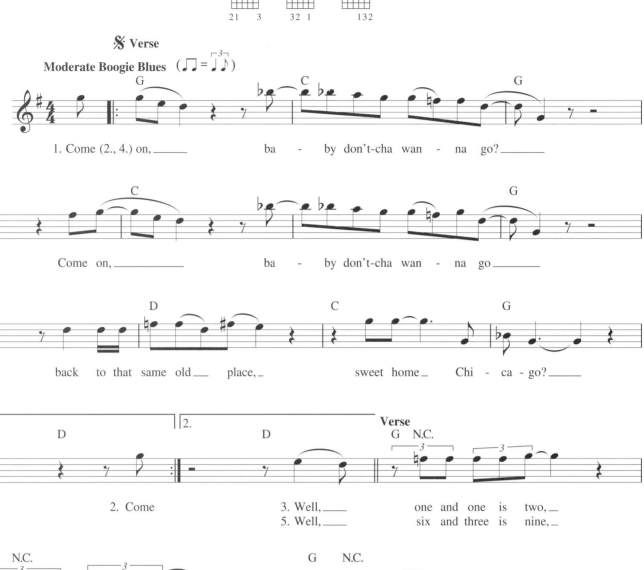

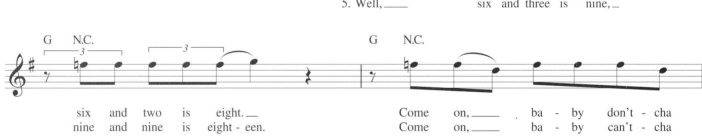

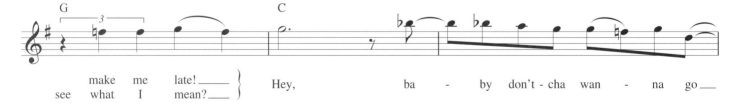

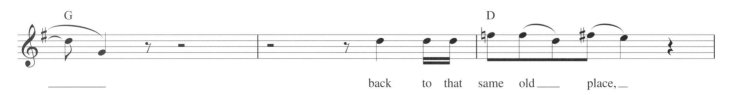

Copyright © (1978), 1990, 1991 Lehsem II, LLC and Claud L. Johnson
Administered by Music & Media International, Inc.
International Copyright Secured   All Rights Reserved

Tutti Frutti

Words and Music by Little Richard Penniman and Dorothy La Bostrie

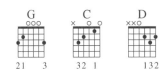

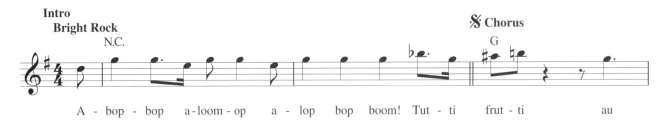

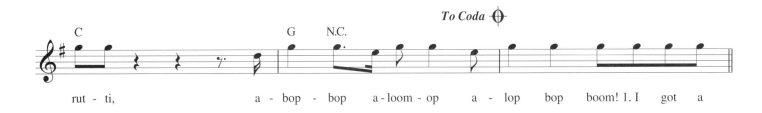

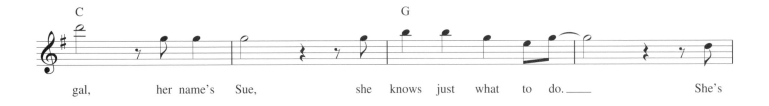

Copyright © 1955, 1956 Sony/ATV Songs LLC
Copyright Renewed
All Rights Administered by Sony/ATV Music Publishing, 8 Music Square West, Nashville, TN 37203
International Copyright Secured   All Rights Reserved

Additional Lyrics

2., 3. I got a gal, her name's Daisy,
She almost drives me crazy.
I got a gal, her name's Daisy,
She almost drives me crazy.
She knows how to love me, yes, indeed.
Boy, you don't know what you do to me.

The Twist

Words and Music by Hank Ballard

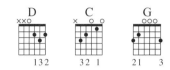

Intro
Moderately fast

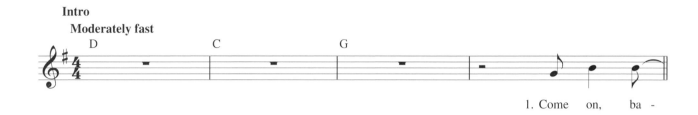

1. Come on, ba-

Verse

-by,   let's do   the   twist.   Come on, ba-

2., 3. *See additional lyrics*

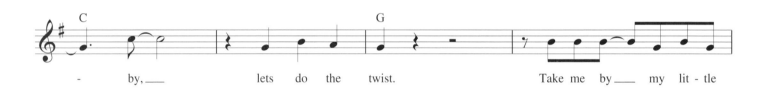

-by, ___   lets do the twist.   Take me by ___ my   lit-tle

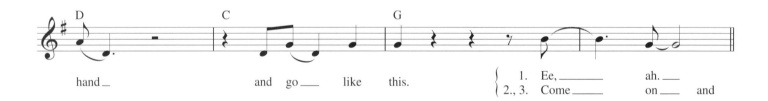

hand ___   and go ___ like   this.

1. Ee, ___   ah. ___
2., 3. Come ___   on ___ and

Chorus

Twist,   babe, ___   ba - by, twist.   Woo, ___
twist,   yeah, ___

4. *Instrumental*

___   yeah, ___   just ___ like

Copyright © 1958 by Fort Knox Music Inc. and Trio Music Company, Inc.
Copyright Renewed
International Copyright Secured   All Rights Reserved
Used by Permission

this.　　Come on,＿ lit - tle miss,＿　　　　and do＿ the

twist.　　　　　2. My　dad - dy　is　sleep - Ee,　ah. ＿＿

Saxophone Solo

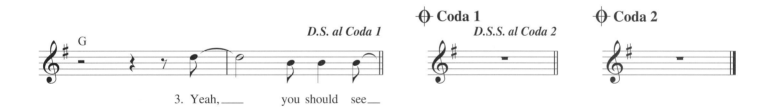

3. Yeah, ＿ you should see ＿

Additional Lyrics

2. My daddy is sleepin' and mama ain't around.
　Yeah, daddy's just sleepin' and mama ain't around.
　We're gonna twist, a twist, a twistin',
　Till we tear the house down.

3. Yeah, you should see my little sis.
　You should see my, my little sis.
　She really knows how to rock,
　She knows how to twist.

Twist and Shout

Words and Music by Bert Russell and Phil Medley

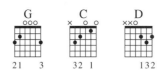

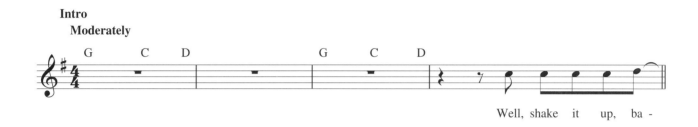

Intro
Moderately

Well, shake it up, ba-

𝄋 Chorus

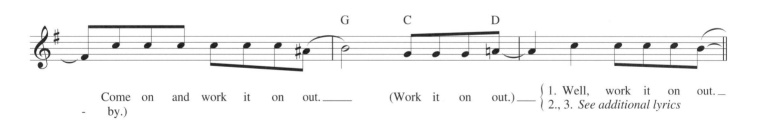

-by, __ now. (Shake it up, ba - by.) Twist and shout. __ (Twist and shout.) __

__ Come on, come on, __ come on, __ come on, ba - by, __ now. (Come on, ba-

Come on and work it on out. __ (Work it on out.) {1. Well, work it on out. __
- by.) {2., 3. *See additional lyrics*

Verse

G   C   D   G   C   D

_____ (Work it on out.) __ You know you look so good. __ (Look so good.) __ You know you got me

Copyright © 1960, 1964 Sony/ATV Songs LLC, Unichappell Music Inc. and Sloopy II Music
Copyright Renewed
All Rights on behalf of Sony/ATV Songs LLC Administered by Sony/ATV Music Publishing, 8 Music Square West, Nashville, TN 37203
International Copyright Secured   All Rights Reserved

go - in', now. (Got me goin'.)__ Just like I knew you would.__ (Like I knew you would.)__

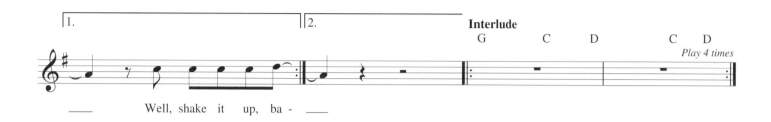

Interlude

G C D C D

Play 4 times

__ Well, shake it up, ba -__

D.S. al Coda

Ah. Ah. Ah. Ah. Ah._____ Shake it up, ba -

Coda

Outro

G C D

__ Well, shake it, shake it, shake it, ba - by, now.__ (Shake it up, ba -

G C D

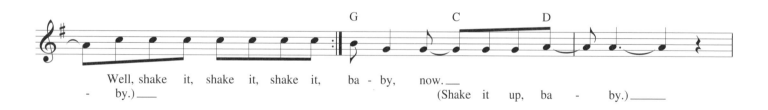

Well, shake it, shake it, shake it, ba - by, now. __ (Shake it up, ba - by.)_____
- by.)__ (Shake it up, ba - by.)_____

N.C. G

Ah. Ah. Ah. Ah.

Additional Lyrics

2., 3. You know you twist, little girl. (Twist little girl.)
You know you twist so fine. (Twist so fine.)
Come on and twist a little closer, now. (Twist a little closer.)
And let me know that you're mine. (Let me know you're mine.)

Werewolves of London

Words and Music by Warren Zevon, Robert Wachtel and LeRoy Marinel

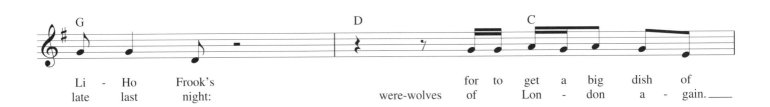

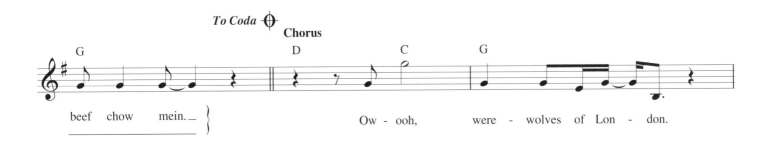

© 1978, 1979 EMI VIRGIN MUSIC LTD. and TINY TUNES MUSIC
All Rights for EMI VIRGIN MUSIC LTD. Controlled and Administered by EMI VIRGIN SONGS, INC.
All Rights for TINY TUNES MUSIC Administered by MUSIC & MEDIA INTERNATIONAL
All Rights Reserved   International Copyright Secured   Used by Permission

Ow - ooh._____

Ow - ooh,   were - wolves of Lon - don.

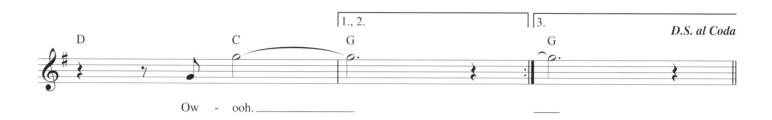

1., 2.   **3.**   *D.S. al Coda*

Ow - ooh._____   ____

Coda

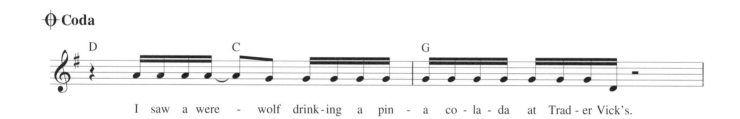

I saw a were - wolf drink-ing a pin - a co - la - da at Trad - er Vick's.

Outro

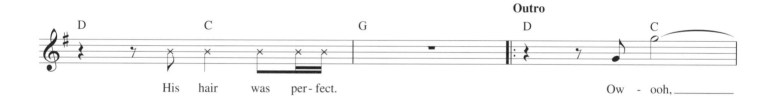

His   hair   was   per - fect.   Ow - ooh,_____

Repeat and fade

_____   were - wolves____ of Lon - don.

Additional Lyrics

3. He's been a hairy-handed gent who ran amok in Kent.
   Lately he's been overheard in Mayfair.
   You'd better stay away from him; he'll rip your lungs out, Jim.
   I'd like to meet his tailor.

4. Well, I saw Lon Chaney walking with the queen,
   Doing the werewolves of London.
   I saw Lon Chaney, Jr. walking with the queen,
   Doing the werewolves of London.
   I saw a werewolf drinking a pina colada at Trader Vick's.
   His hair was perfect.

Wooly Bully

Words and Music by Domingo Samudio

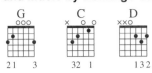

Pre-Intro
Moderately

Spoken: Uno, dos.   One, two, tres, quattro.   Hey.

𝄋 Intro

Wooly Bully.   Watch it, now. Watch it.   Here he comes.   Here he comes.

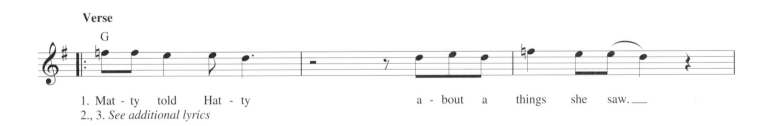

Watch it, now. He'll get you.

Verse

1. Mat - ty told Hat - ty   a - bout a things she saw. __
2., 3. *See additional lyrics*

Had two big horns __   and a wool - y jaw. __ Wool - y

Copyright © 1964 Sony/ATV Songs LLC and Embassy Music Corporation
Copyright Renewed
All Rights on behalf of Sony/ATV Songs LLC Administered by Sony/ATV Music Publishing, 8 Music Square West, Nashville, TN 37203
International Copyright Secured   All Rights Reserved

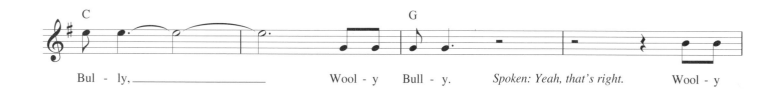

Bul - ly, _____ Wool - y Bull - y. *Spoken: Yeah, that's right.* Wool - y

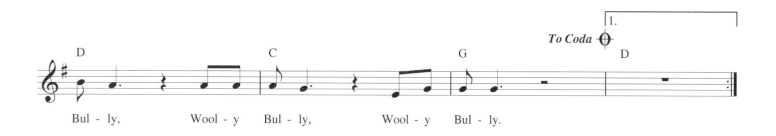

1.

To Coda ⊕

Bul - ly, Wool - y Bul - ly, Wool - y Bul - ly.

2. **Pre-Intro** *D.S. al Coda*

⊕ **Coda**

Outro

Spoken: He got it. He got it.

Additional Lyrics

2. Hatty told Matty
   Let's don't take no chance.
   Let's not be L 7.
   Come and learn to dance.
   Wooly Bully, Wooly Bully,
   Wooly Bully, Wooly Bully, Wooly Bully.
   Spoken: Watch it, now. Watch it, watch it, watch it.

3. Matty told Hatty
   That's the thing to do.
   Get yo' someone really
   To pull the wool with you.
   Wooly Bully, Wooly Bully,
   Wooly Bully, Wooly Bully, Wooly Bully.
   Spoken: Watch it, now. Watch it. Here he comes.

Yakety Yak

Words and Music by Jerry Leiber and Mike Stoller

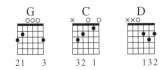

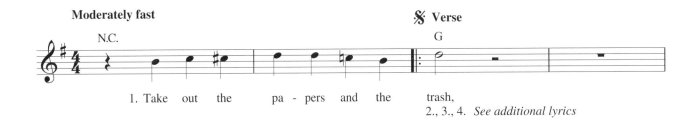

1. Take out the pa - pers and the trash,
2., 3., 4. *See additional lyrics*

or you don't get no spend - ing cash.

If you don't scrub that kitch - en floor,

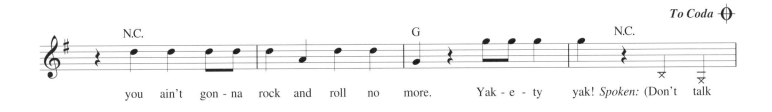

you ain't gon - na rock and roll no more. Yak - e - ty yak! *Spoken:* (Don't talk

back.) 2. Just fin - ish clean - in' up ___ your back.)

Copyright © 1958 (Renewed) JERRY LEIBER MUSIC and MIKE STOLLER MUSIC
All Rights Reserved

Saxophone Solo

4. Don't you give me no dirt - y

Coda

Outro

back.)   Yak - e - ty   yak, ___   yak - e - ty   yak! _

Repeat and fade

Yak - e - ty   yak,   yak - e - ty

Additional Lyrics

2. Just finish cleanin' up your room.
   Let's see that dust fly with that broom.
   Get all that garbage out of sight,
   Or you don't go out Friday night.
   Yakety yak! *Spoken: (Don't talk back.)*

3. You just put on your coat and hat,
   And walk yourself to the laundromat.
   And when you finish doing that,
   Bring in the dog and put out the cat.
   Yakety yak! *Spoken: (Don't talk back.)*

4. Don't you give me no dirty looks.
   Your father's hip; he knows what cooks.
   Just tell your hoodlum friends outside,
   You ain't got time to take a ride.
   Yakety yak! *Spoken: (Don't talk back.)*

When Will I Be Loved

Words and Music by Phil Everly

Additional Lyrics

3., 4. I've been cheated,
Been mistreated.
When will I be loved?

Copyright © 1960 (Renewed 1988) by Acuff-Rose Music, Inc.
All Rights Reserved   Used by Permission